Praise for

EVANESCENT CREATURE

"Shavawn M. Berry's verse in *Evanescent Creature: Poems & Meditations*, forges nuanced pathways into ancient themes surrounding both the ubiquitous and hidden nature of the feminine. Her masterfully poised hymns to the cyclical nature of life overflow with possibilities. We witness Berry step into the prophetic role imparted upon her by a Grandmother Spider in one of her poems, and powerfully spin evocative personal narratives, at times laced with delightful didactic panache.

"Ironically, there is nothing ephemeral about the effect of reading Berry's poetry collection, which lingers with the reader long after its ingestion, like scents inhabit ether on a midsummer night.

"An unmistakably dazzling debut!"

—CATHERINE L. SCHWEIG, Founder and Director of Journey of the Heart: Women's Spiritual Poetry Project, Chief Editor, *Goddess: When She Rules* (Golden Dragonfly Press, 2018)

"In *Evanescent Creature*, we are invited to share Berry's invocations to memory, reflection, awareness. Berry's words draw in the senses and nature to give us gentle snapshots of insight. Her verse is delicate, circling the archetypal journey of women, and we feel the relationship with souls that persist, appear, and ponder."

—SARAH AMIRA DE LA GARZA, Southwest Borderlands Scholar at Arizona State University and author of *María Speaks: Journeys into the Mysteries of the Mother in My Life as a Chicana*

"Leap without looking. *Evanescent Creature* is a collection of shiver-inducing poems and meditations that will leave you to ponder, wonder, and marvel as you wander through the almost synesthesia-inducing warm embrace of words."

—DARRAGHA FOSTER, Author of *Love's Second Sight*

EVANESCENT CREATURE

FIRST PRINT EDITION, March 2023
FIRST EBOOK EDITION, April 2023

ISBN: 978–1–7370545–8–0

Library of Congress Control Number: 2023932058

Printed on acid-free paper supplied by a Forest Stewardship Council-certified
provider. First published in the United States of America by Golden
Dragonfly Press, 2023.

For permission requests, write to the author:
www.thewonderlandfiles.com
www.goldendragonflypress.com

SHAVAWN M. BERRY

Evanescent Creature

POEMS & MEDITATIONS

2023

GOLDEN DRAGONFLY PRESS

Amherst, Massachusetts

In memory of my Nana, Sarah Trelle Moon
Poet Laureate of the Class of 1927 at Barnard Women's College
who instilled in me a life-long love for Rilke, Tagore, & Gibran

With reverence for my father, Wallace Earle Berry
June 29, 1926–March 18, 2003

In honor of my warrior of a mother, Amanda Moore Berry

When sleeping women wake,
Mountains move.

—CHINESE PROVERB

Contents

Crone 107

Credits/Acknowledgements/Gratitude

Many of these poems have been published in creative writing & literary magazines over the years. Blessings and thanks to them all for their encouragement and support. Some of the versions in this book differ from the originally published versions.

Blue Angel Writes to Tell Me—Synapse Magazine

San Juan Island's Youngest Daughter—Synapse Magazine

Granddaddy—Synapse Magazine

Unraveling Baba Yaga, Journey of Heart: Women's Spiritual Poetry

Off with Her Head: The Dangerous, Divine Feminine Responds—The Urban Howl

Feral Child—Westview: A Journal of Western Oklahoma

Descent Into Madness—Westview: A Journal of Western Oklahoma

This Way—Olentangy Review

Wolf One—Black Fox Literary Magazine

Día de los Muertos—Trickster Magazine

Self Portrait—Trickster Magazine

What I See—Huffpo 50

Ephemera—The Cancer Poetry Project 2 (Anthology)

Hibakusha—Sable Books' Anthology, Red Sky—Poetry on the Global Epidemic of Violence Against Women

Blue Forest Elegy—Meridian Anthology of Contemporary Poetry

Dreaming in Karbala—Poet Lore

Magical/Wounded/Timeless Child

As she sleeps, she takes on an animal softness
And the trees become centaurs

In her dreams giraffes drink from the hotel toilet
and a gazelle curls up like an acorn on her bed

The Fool

Your journey into a hinterland
begins. Leap without looking.
The summit's in sight.
Green rivers of time
and space uncoil below you.

You can do anything
And go anywhere,
There are no limits
To what is possible
Or probable.

And the universe sees you
Tiny insect in its care,
Ready and willing to
Reinvent yourself,
To re-envision your life.

Open the portal

And go.

Feral Child

For Sabrina, at 13

The thistles are crackling in their coats
Calling you with the wind toward the Witch—
Woman's cabin and this hilltop's sharp peak.
Up here, you can see miles of Puget Sound
Curling around the green carcass of San Juan Island.
Up here, the sky lifts for leagues above your eyes,
Opening your chest, charring your senses

Like sunflowers growing on Hannah Road.
The strong basket you carry on your arm
Slowly fills with brown eggs, a fallen bird's nest,
Blackberries and salmonberries.
You watch hawks circle, wing patterns
a languid oval in the azure sky,
Your face a book of secret wishes.

You have fallen into a place I cannot follow.
As you climb, I see more clearly
The child being overtaken by the young woman
You turn to me, the sun catching
Rivers of color in your long blond braid,
Wholly unaware of the light that spills from you,
Your dusky face an unfettered tangle of morning glory
Pale and lovely in the salty, still air.

The Sun

Born with the sun
in Aries in the 9th house

Of adventure,
travel, higher

education, and fierce
independence

With Leo rising like
The sun in the 1st house

Your personality
Your fierce

Sense of truth
Flaring & flaming

your longing to map
Foreign countries

And leave the hermitage
Of your fragile

unbound
essential, wildish nature

Has caused you
To remain unsettled

Unbroken &
Unabashedly

Yourself.

San Juan Island's Youngest Daughter

For Tuck

I rip open your latest letter
The love I feel for you
Billowing in my chest like cool salt air.
You write, "I miss you a lot," in your crayon scrawl.
I remember the thump of your heart
as I hugged you last August,
Tickling you through your smock,
while you giggled uncontrollably,
laughter echoing through the house.

It had rained, left us to our books, drawings,
Left us to break beans from the food co-op.
We sat in the rocker by the wood stove
Inhaling the buttery smell of your mother's bread.
I worked the snarls out of your wavy gold hair,
And slowly braided it down your back.
You sat so still—Patient for a seven-year-old,
Sighed a little, talked to the cats mewling at our feet.
We sang ditties as Sabrina's chickens prattled

Under the pines outside the kitchen door.
Occasionally they would push the door open
And wander in, until you ran at them, stomping and
Shouting: "Shoo, stupid chickens!"
Scattering them back into the yard,
Their shiny eyes bulging,
useless wings flapping.
After I finished your hair
We went over the ridge to the goat shed,

Tied your goats to graze.
You rubbed their stubby horns, scratched their chins,
As they munched and cawed at you thoughtfully.

"They don't like the rain," you explained.
"Next year, they'll have kids."
That night your mother and mine
And we three daughters
Ate a spread of curry chicken, rice, bread, salad
And sparkling cider by candlelight.

A mile below us lights bobbed on the Sound,
The clouds cleared, and stars speckled above.
We listened to the owls until after midnight.
Now, almost a year later
You write and ask me to visit again.
Your invitation opens to me like a yellow poppy,
Like your blackberry-stained face did last summer
As we ate our way home through a roadside of brambles.
"Come in July. My birthday is in July,"

You tell me,
reaching out with the words,
Daring me to skip and cartwheel,
To jump rope with kelp on the beach.
Keep that sand under your nails for me.
Let the wind tangle up your hair
And I will comb it out for you.
Sleep with your favorite dog for a pillow.
Don't wear socks, ever.

I love your voice calling me
back to Friday Harbor,
To alfalfa fields,
smokey clothes,
unbaked bread.
I'll come back
for that part of myself
I left dancing under a pine,
High above the Strait of Juan de Fuca.

Meditation on Trees

Birch sap stains the
  Nests of broken, white branches
    Gold-winged, otherworldly
      Why does the wind
        make the trees rustle & chatter?
          Where do crickets learn to sing?

Dangerous Creature

You can make yourself
disappear, at will.
You've always been able to.
You possess the capacity
to blend in, like bark
Or pebbles, or sea glass.

You can shape-shift to
swallow what surrounds you
Or allow yourself
to be swallowed whole like
rare white-whales swallow mermen,
krill, mackerel, and plankton.

You can wrap yourself in
rust and feathers.
You can rise and bellow,
shattering the chalice
of chaste silence.
Sea grit and half shell

Tar, black sand,
and sandpiper—
Starless still night
You can walk
even though
your legs are broken;

You can speak
With no tongue;
You are a deep well of numinous
Fireflies & nocturnal light.
You stand at the door
Waiting for me to let you in.

Dendrophile

She talks to trees, incessantly,
And listens, her ear to tree's trunk
As its roots chatter &
Move through the wet ground

She touches bark, burls
Tender leaves—
Trims suckers
On low hanging branches

each Spring
as soon as they bud.
She figures that any sentient thing
standing stone-still

Growing up and out and out
Filling the air again, and again
Without moving to another state or city
Without crossing an ocean to be anywhere

Other than where it is:
Is a wise being, a soul constellation
A celestial time marker,
An enlightened one.

Awakening

Outside, speckled in sunlight,
You whirl in the tree swing,
Watch the light change
from under its soft shade

In your head
You write God a letter today
You scratch it tenderly
into your translucent skin

You use a roaring voice
As it
Suddenly emerges
from its chrysalis

You sing it out loudly
And see everything begin to glow
You hear sweet crickets
Click and clack their small feet

As everything begins to thrum & sing

Rooms & Windows

What part of me is
needing a home,
a rest, a chance to
Cut open these
rooms & windows
Scissors sharp
to the utter delight
of cutting and pasting,

collaging &
paper dreaming,
to talking cat &
dancing dog,
to asking cottonwoods
my most pressing questions

Why did our dog have to die?
How do my legs carry me?
Where did grandaddy go when he left us?
Why do we have to take baths?
What makes water slip through my fingers?
How did I come to be?

Photo by Harry Ray Topping, 1940

Granddaddy

I

Granddad was born in Lincoln, Nebraska
Raised by his father,
Thought his long dead mother was a saint.
He named my momma after his mother.
She was the only one of his children
Who never felt the sting of his hand slapping her face.

Granddad was a gypsy
Who thrived on moving every year.
This year Seattle, next year Flagstaff, or Winslow.
When he first married Nana
They lived in a trailer in the desert.
Every day when he left for work,
He locked her inside with their children,
Because his first wife ran away from him.

Granddad paced the desert carrying a forked stick
To smash the head of any rattler that crossed his path.
He surveyed the dry terrain, searched for unusual rocks
To throw in his rock polisher,
Photographed every spring's ruby cactus flowers.
His photographs appeared in *Arizona Highways*.
He took hundreds of color slides of his children,
Cursing as the flies buzzed around him:
Stand still, damn it! And don't move!

Momma and her sisters would whimper
And wipe their noses on their dresses.
His youngest daughter smashed him over the head
With a cast iron skillet

While he was trying
To throw Nana down a flight of stairs.

Nana left Granddaddy in 1949.
She packed up the children and moved from
Winslow, Arizona to Burien, Washington
By Greyhound Bus one day while he was at work.

II

Granddaddy came to visit when I was seven.
He bought me a bike and a bow and arrow set.
He showed me blue and silver stones,
Chunks of polished granite,
Huge rings of keys.
He drove an old beater of a truck,
Boasted how he'd driven on the shoulder of the road
From California up the coast
Doing 40 miles per hour.
(His license had been suspended several years before.)

He was dusty and oily, his white hair slicked back.
He walked with a shuffle,
Never took a bath.
After he washed his neck with a musty washcloth
He sat me on his lap and said:
"Don't I smell good?"
While I tried not to breathe.
He gave me a thousand dollars confederate money
Told me not to spend it in one place.
Over dinner, he fought with momma,
Kicked our dog for barking.
I hid outside on the tree swing,
Watched the blueness of the sky
Filtering through summer leaves,
Hummed a song to myself.

III

Granddaddy died in Quartzsite, Arizona.
He sat down in a yard chair outside his truck
And fell asleep.
There was no funeral.
He was cremated and left in Arizona.
We sold his truck.
Months later I pulled his rock collection
Off the shelf in the living room
And fingered the stones in each box.

I rubbed the smooth and rough stones
Of turquoise, sandstone, fool's gold, crystal, quartz—
Thought about the last thing he said to me:
"I'll dance with you on your wedding day."

IV

The bike Granddad gave me lies kicked over
In our backyard, rusty, tires flat.
It's been years since I last rode it.
These days I send my memories of Granddaddy
Skipping out over the ocean
Like flat gray stones, to sink.
Momma has exiled him to the desert
To become part of the fiery sky at dusk.
We remember him when Nana's Christmas cactus
Blooms in each new year.
We drink coffee,
and sometimes raise our cups
As if in a toast,
The silence says:
Here's to that son-of-a-bitch, my father.

We gulp the coffee down,
Feel the scalding liquid
Burn in our bellies.

Santos

She paints words with her index finger
Her hat is a nest for magpies

She smells of corn masa and raw milk
Red rocks ring, hum—

Their voices bell-clear
The Santo speaks to her

From where it hangs on the wall,
Recalling its time in a carver's hands

In her dreams rattlesnakes can talk
And a dark sedan idles at the curb,

Clouding the basement of her childhood

Ode to a Seedling

You fearlessly imagine your life,
A weathered map folded up,
taking you wherever you want to go.

You carry it in a red velvet purse,
Like a fragile robin's egg,
A talisman, or a compass pointing North.

You toss its seeds
in the rust-colored dirt
in your garden outback—

& You water it and
watch the ground
crack into fissures of green

It sprouts, a smear of purple and fuchsia,
Revealing the leafy stems of who you once were.

Starlings

At night, you recall
their fierce gaze

When they faced
north to find you, &

they slept in the
crook of your back.

They lit things on fire just
To watch them burn.

They rooted their feet
Inside your head,

Like a buck's antlers
Filled with starlings.

Dharma Girl

How can I find the quiet forest in my chest?

I

My sister died in October 1955.
She was 18 days old. Born blue,
her heart a bittersweet raisin in her chest,
My mother named her Roxanne.

II

In a rush of birth waters, a salt lick
Spread on the sheet under my mother's pelvis.
Outside, red throated hummingbirds rose and fell on rivers of wind,
As I slipped into life soft as a ripe pear.

III

No human starfish, swirling, dancing
burrowed into my solar plexus.
I birthed no daughter.
This red thread breaks *with me*.

IV

The grief of losing a child
still marks Momma's face at 87.
The small ghost of her first baby
rests her head on my mother's shoulder, even now.

V

I am the girl that lived.
Doctor Buell laid me on my mother's chest
As soon as I took my first breath.
My ear nestled against Momma's ribs

As the book of my life opened.

Grandmother Spider

"You were born with big power.
Big medicine," Spider tells me
Strands of her sticky, gossamer web
Floating down from the ceiling

as she dangles above my bed.
"You wield big magic.
You must use lush words
gathered in your root chakra

Waiting for you to cough them up
And weave your story.
You were not meant to stand silent,
While spirit speaks through you

While the voices of the ancestors,
the warrior women & world-weary witches
who gave rise to your life
Drowned in icy ponds

Stones filling their pockets as
Your people watched
In mute horror."
Your destiny is as a Spinner,

A Sower of tiny stories
A teller of tall tales
that give the world
Letters and syllables

Consonants and vowels
Leaves and roots
That fill the pages that
Will save this world

and the next; the ghost world
and the astral world,
The human world,
and the feral world.

You were born with big power

Use it.

Selkie

Whale song follows you—
      even on dry land

You trail kelp, sea
      anemones, and salt water

Mermaid,

    Water sprite,

        shining dolphinfish

Silver Holy Water

Pebbles form concentric patterns
under her feet. She says a mantra
softly, savoring each prayer bead as she touches it.

She drinks from a cup of silver holy water,
counts her steps as she walks
the circumference of a labyrinth.

Back in her simple room, she writes
His name in ink and water—her finger her instrument—
Tracing the memory of the curve of his back.

Outside, fields of Indian paintbrush bend and sway,
heavy with the soft thrum of bees. Clouds spill shadows
into the kitchen as an ant colony chews

On sweet meats and cakes dripping with honey.
Just out of sight, a mute child
stands in the courtyard, watching,
marmalade cat flung over her shoulder,
belly sleek as a seal pelt.

Maiden, Lost & Found

The fork and spoon party with the good china
As she conceals her tail under her street clothes

The Archer

She pulls the arrow from her chest
The porch swing where they sit

Creaks in the cool breeze
Evergreens hover, sway

She dreams of sandwiches full of babies
As a pale slipper moon watches her

Night flowers open &
She runs her tongue over his mouth

Feels his warm sap rise
Her face coloring a flagrant pastel

Like one of Degas' whores:
Hello my purr willow

My slice of scars
My soft belly finger wag

Amelia Circumnavigates the Globe

As a girl, I loved her jaunty
leather flight jacket and goggles

Scarf flying beside her
on violent currents of wind

Her small plane carrying her across
Oceans, countries, time zones—I

Read her biography twice, before I turned 8
Poured over *Life Magazine*

With her on the cover
Mapped out all her journeys

And wondered
how she got so brave

So, unruly
So unwilling to toe the line

I admired her gumption
And her gall

Her poise
And her sense of purpose

Her short bob &
the freckles dotting her nose—

I followed her fierce ending
As she checked in

One final time
And then fell off radar

On one of the last legs
Of her flight

To circumnavigate
The globe

The Hierophant

To conjure her
Laden with lapis lazuli
Petals littering her hair
Scepter firmly in her hand

Call on the Owl moon
On the elf owl, the burrowing owl
The barn owl, the chicks
Tucked in under

Their mother's feathery breast
Send in Sophia's wisdom
The sign of the crescent moon
The shadow of a hawk's wing

The knowledge of the temple
Of the black Madonna
Of Isis and Osiris
And the pools

Along the Nile
Give me eyes to see
Truth, strangeness
Wickedness, wisdom.

Give me the keys
You've cut your teeth on.

Guidance from Darkness

Enchantment is the oldest form of healing.

A hypnotic voice sends me a dream
Delivers a murky pool of
slippery water & little to no light

American eels slither past me,
Smelling like brine & fetid
bracken water; once there

I morph into a seal-skin woman
into a fish-maiden
Kelp hair streaming down my back

The voice admonishes me:
Turn over every stone to
See what's underneath

See where the roots of your shame,
your madness, your numinous self
Took shape

See the places where the umbilicus
of your sense of invisibility seeded, flourished
Look at all of it

And

Dismantle it.

A Big Fucking Fence

You are a gleaming, raw
Open wound

A tear in the gauze of fabric of the world
Hanging in the morning air

You feel everything
The rush of grief, exhaustion

Overwhelm
Chaos

Nearly knocking you sideways
When you pass strangers in the street

You are permeable
Borderless

You won't learn defense
Until you've endured years of defenselessness

And finally, you'll take down the sign
Above your head

That says:
Open for business—

Listening.
Here for only you.

And trade it
For boundaries

And a

    big

        fucking

           fence.

Tattoo

I'm holding my breath,
lungs catching fire
Holding, counting, longing
As though if I take a breath,

If I dare breathe in
These flaming trees or sweet crocus
My chest will break open
And a murder of crows will

Rise up in black furrows
And ensnare the quiet blue above
They'll build a home in my hair
And unravel whatever it is that

Makes it palatable to be *less than whole*
Less than OK. If I release these charcoal nightbirds
They'll stain me with their permanent ink,
They'll tattoo my brokenness all over my body

And I'll become a set of dirty linens
Lying still on the floor

Wolf One

The moon's reflection
In a martini glass

A willow's branch
Sweeping through a stream

Our Lady of the Milky Breasts
The white fountain, opaque thigh

He etches his name
In the glass of her gaze

His cuticles bleed as he
Chews his hands raw

The line of her neck
Curves like a black swan

He licks a circle, a nest,
A breaking point on her back

Her white teeth glisten
As she bares her fangs

96

For M

These remnant days, scraps
Woven with sea glass & sparrow's wings

I sift through words carefully,
Dress up dead language on a moonless night.

That final morning, following your russet river
I heard my blood slow and stop.

It pooled in the blue baskets of my wrists,
awaiting further instructions.

There are 96 words for love.

      96.

      You conjure each one.

What's Left Behind

We must be willing to let go of the life we have planned, to accept the life that is waiting for us. —Joseph Campbell

Everywhere, reminders: half-filled journal, coal-black teapot, French Press, New York Times' crossword puzzle marked in careful handwriting, and, of course, the letters, letters on white vellum, words that quicken her pulse. His living remnants stretch out on loose cots, laze on feather beds, permanent house guests napping inside her right atrium, left ventricle, tricuspid valve. They ride blood rivers, smack rocks, uproot trees, casting shadows in the mud-thick currents. She rocks in a torn-up chair—a girl again—she rocks & tones & coughs up pebbles. She knows she will smother under these pillows if she doesn't wake up. *Ventricular septum; superior vena cava; coronary artery; mitral valve*; she names her parts—knows each piece floats inside a fragile ruby, a bee's nest under her left rib.

She still sees his outline on the bed sheets.

Reminders.

Everywhere.

The Handless Maiden

She needs to scratch an itch,
To stick in his craw,
To find a sluice his boat might open

Otherworldly feelings stir
Watch a nosegay unfold
Awaiting, re-making, reimagining her life

A Devil's bargain takes her hands
Severs her unhanded heart
He gives her tiny horses with sweet grass tails

Her silver dress spins and turns in on itself
Along the skin of her consciousness
A blue crone catches fire, a pearl in her aching, small shoe

Sea Anemone

Tides blow right through her
Slide sharp across her tongue

Salt coats her gleaming skin &
Pulls her body through a wormhole

As the moon rises
the water carves image, word

into driftwood and sea glass
Worn soft by sand and salt

Still, she floats,
A silver mermaid

Under Castor & Pollux,
Under the star-poked ceiling
of an ocean cathedral

Blackbird

Tremendous wings
break the skin
of your shoulder blades

Slowly, you peel away
Your shoes, your dark tights
Your bra and high-waisted underwear

You unzip your dress

     & watch me

      as it falls around you

       Like a blackbird's body

Meditation on Celestial Things

A dress of stars

    pulling the sky

    across the world,

    assuages my grief &

        stops the forest of bitterness

          threatening to devour

            me

The Collector

She wears a mantle of pink oleanders
He piles river-smooth rocks on her chest
Leaves worry stones in the cradles of her palms
Notices an anklet of ink circling her calf

Sweat traces the jagged curve of his spine
Fire ants surface to drink as
He arranges her earthy bed carefully
And readies her for burial

He places broken bird's eggs,
Wet moss, silver-green twigs

Just so

He keeps his trophies
Tiny reminders:
a button, an eyelash,
a gold crucifix

Manzanitas scour the air above her
Feathering out like Medusa's snakes
Constellations of leaves
Trail seedpods on the soft ground

Only now, does he notice her birch-like feet
And their tender, white roots

Snapshots

Aperture

Her lungs ache
As she runs from the Tube
Sunflowers wrapped in newsprint
Tucked under her arm
Coat soaked through

Focus

As she unlocks
the door to her flat
a hand grabs
her neck, shoves
into wall,
steel thumb
circling one areola

As she's ripped wide open

Shutter

While reading
the morning newspaper,
she sobs—
Over Sharia law,
Which forces women
to wear chadors
in 120-degree weather,
Requires them to be
submissive, pure, honorable,
Girls as young as nine

available to their husbands—
at all times—
even while riding a camel

Advance

The next morning, she boards a train headed for the Isle of Skye.

She never tells anyone.

On BBC Radio she hears Ayatollah Khomeini's sexual advice to Muslim men, reported by a staid British news announcer:

A man can have sex with animals such as sheep, cows, camels, and so on. However, he should kill the animal afterward.[1]

Her tea tastes like kerosene.

Water Bath

She watches as the desert floods
Summer monsoon; thunder-split sky

She longs to stand in a downpour
Bask in the hard mineral grit of rainwater

Sees the hours curl in & stretch out
Still smelling fetid breath on her face

Light

Palo Verdes bend over the street
their smooth branches
dusted with pastel leaves

Speckled with light
She walks home,
A lone cactus wren
calling her name—

Dry

She has no tears, salt.

She hangs herself up like
A stained bedsheet.

She imagines her mother
in Dresden during the war

Bomb fragments slicing
her skin to the bone

She dreams she's there,
swallowing fire

[1] Khomeini Quote: Don't Get Lucky, Get Smart by Alan Cohen, p. 208.

Begonias

Wrens stand at attention,
Feet grasping wires strung mid-air

The trapeze artist flies
a lemon-yellow kite,

In her pocket, a chipping sparrow's nest
In her hand, a lizard's egg

She feels rivers in her blood going dry
As a swan tucks a new set of keys in her pocket

Clouds slide together mingling juices
Their blush faces flawless begonias

Ephemera

In memory of Maricela Ochoa-Henderson

Your defective breasts are gone
Replaced by a fresh set, small areolas
Decorating your flat, creamy chest

You smell like tortillas, corn mush
The cremated dust of
your bones and skin belong

To some other girl; someone
else's dismantled body
sits on a shelf at your folk's house

Brown-black hair frames your face,
a dark tide of seaweed rushing
past your neck, collar bone, shoulders

You've been dead a week
when you visit, a cherry-colored scarf
knotted at your throat

You aren't gone,
just between adventures
Abre la puerta—Open the door

You sit next to me, naked,
no more than 20-years-old,
Unencumbered
by the rot and shit
and bile of stage IV cancer
You hold my wrists hard
as I fight to wake,

Try to say what I— *Mi amiga*
Your skin is warm, salty

Everything's rustling
with scattered light
I feel your breath on my face

You speak to me in Spanish,
whole phrases float like
iridescent hummingbirds,

Syllables fall open,

calla lilies flush with blooms

St. Theresa

When she recalls her milky face
She thinks of roses—
American beauties &
Blooms the color of clotted cream,

Flowers tinged with
orange pink edges
As the fecund smell of fertilizer
Rises off the wet ground

She thinks of cloisters and the sun fading
As church bells peal, a lone taper lit
For vespers, the soft clicking of beads
As brides of Christ kneel and pray

She thinks of a whoosh of feathers
As she floats above the stone floor
Weightless, effortless
Eyes flooded with tears, lips, stained rubies

She hears whispers as the
Rain calls her by her given name &
Sparrows speak to her, air clouded with
Falling stars:

Holy, holy—exalted
pure.

Two White Tulips

For T

You listen to me,
deeply—without
needing to fix me

You allow
my beautiful mess
You simply listen

You let me stand
inside my silence
Without needing to

fill the air with sound
You give me space
between the notes

You don't fill me up
You know
I am already full

You love my fragile bones,
my pale skin, the
scar on my nose & under my lip

You see *me*, not your own reflection

You gift me with the green stems of myself

Yellow Snakes

The husk of her voice pebbles his nightmare
He polishes crescent moons on his fingernails
Picks his cuticles until they bleed

Cicadas buzz and swim in the damp air
As he watches her,
he imagines a newborn baby

At dusk, he remembers nothing
but the warm furnace of her mouth
Her hair, a riot of yellow snakes

Meditation on Embodiment

How does one stay embodied,

        grounded,

            present,

                during sex?

    Isn't it

      Better to float away

        like an anemone

           or sea star?

Incantation

Deer munch on twigs
bright with cherry blossoms

A thimble of white wings
drag your voice from your throat

You call on your own nature
To fill the vast emptiness you see

You wail, wallow, shimmy
Your teeth like sharp knives

You hiss and snarl
An incantation

As you dance with imaginary starfish
You've called from the sea

The smell of citrus, wood
smoke, & the sound of

a bell ringing, conjuring
a pillow swollen with rain

He hears your siren sound
& sews himself shut

With a needle
and stiff red thread

You ponder the echo
of his voice

You are the radiance you seek

For Jane

You are shimmering tallow, cobalt wings,
a sandalwood heart
You are ruby roses in blushing bloom,
a riot of yellow sunlight touching the dark air with your fragrance
You are sweet sage stinging our eyes, and
Clouds of blue smoke rousing our senses
A fallow field full of dead stars
Slowly dropping to earth
You are the bones of white aspens
now fallen on the forest's floor
You are a darkling angel whose husky voice
dreams this world into being
What would any of us be without you?
You snake through our blood and brine,
leave us inebriated with joy; even in grief, you are there
counting the grace of each hour,
filling us with what it means to be completely alive.

The Good Witch

The tuxedo cat dances a jig under
the eaves of a tilting house, a storm teardown

Good witch, kind witch, bold witch
She's got lavender church-spire eyes

She blushes in her imagined role
as a verdant, Greenleaf bride

She packs his valise full
of sandwiches & poems.

What else could he
Possibly need?

Nearby, soft buds act as landing pads
To a lemon feathered tanager

And Joshua trees beckon you,
Sky the color of a watery cup of coffee

What will she learn today?
What strange blue door will open

And ask her to come inside?

Isis

The sky's a sheaf of unspoken words,

storm gathering,

water falling—

her

dismembered life

surfacing

on the waves

Migrating South

She knew things
between them
were over
when she asked him
what he loved about her
and he said:

I love what you do with your mouth

What she wanted to hear
was that he longed
for every syllable
that fell from her lips
or loved the way her hair
tumbled across
her face while she slept

Instead
he vivisected her
into body parts
tongue
soft palette
throat open
curving swan neck

fingers grasping him hard

his whole body a conflagration

                                       as he watched her work

Hibakusha

For Margie Hunt

Sixty years sat like stones on my chest
Pinned me to the surface of the earth

Let me walk and move and talk
As if I went on living after that day

As though I did not see
The burning air, or smell the radiation fires

Containing women, babies strapped to
Their backs; old men playing cards—

That morning I didn't go to my factory job
Instead, I went with Daddy to his

As I sat—daydreaming—head resting on my warm palm
The sky darkened, turned gold, then imploded

The walls around me fell like toothpicks
Scattered on the floor of our restaurant

Afterward, I walked the streets
With my father, searching for my sister

The ground littered with phosphorescent
Flowers glowing like raw embers

Upon closer inspection, I saw pieces of
Skin and bone, not flowers:

A woman's severed hand,
An ear torn from its socket.

Even as my hair fell out in shanks
I did not cry

Even as my father died of brain cancer
My eyes had no water

Even as my mother bled to death
From one slight bruise on her arm

No rain fell on my cheek
I held my breath, bit my tongue

Until six decades
Left me gulping for air

As one small child,
His black hair cut in the shape

Of a noodle bowl, gifted me
With a strand of flame-colored cranes

So, I might begin,
to remember this clear river inside of me

And finally loosen the broken
Songbird in my throat

Kuan Yin Rides a Dragon

A camelia floating on still water
She calls all errant boats back to shore

She rides an iridescent greening dragon &
Rescues drowning sailors lost at sea

She tucks a glowing embryo inside
Women in lamentation, longing for a child,

Her graceful intervention
Births this & that tender bird

Lotus blossoms open
Rooted in a blood-red tree of life

Lining a coppery womb
Planting her wishes on fecund ground

Rebirth

For Melissa

Buddha says let go.

I pile imaginary stones in front of my gold lacquer altar, scroll splashed with Sanskrit characters, lotus in the center of my life, blooming & seeding simultaneously. Those invisible rocks form a wall, my burdens pinned beneath each one. Candles drip as I count prayer beads, moving from one end to the other, twisting them into a figure eight, the sign of infinity. I slowly chant the liturgy & visualize cherry blossoms falling around me as my prayer ends.

Blue lace agate reminds me of you. I turn the smooth stone against my palm—lavender twilight—striated with small crystal veins. My chest tightens. You've been gone more than two decades.

Remembering that September day, I finger my ribs, wonder how it felt to fall through the air; wonder how it would feel to have a rib bone slice through my liver.

Buddha says let go.

The girl you *were* bled out, Medi-vac chopper blades thrashing in the clear fall air, Puget Sound rippling below.

Buddha says it's your mind that creates this world.

You left *that girl* in a body bag, parked like crumpled linens, outside the morgue.

Whenever you think of her, the child who now breathes in her place, turns her head, hair a snarled stream around her, hears your voice calling

She wonders where that sound begins.

Blue Forest Elegy

I have buried my heart
with its bruised longing for you

In a blue forest, under a bed of twigs
and things that rustle, snap and sing—

Under blinding snow and spring storms,
where rivers of rain will wash it clear of you

I have buried it in a hinterland filled with bones,
Planted it beside the carcasses

of cats and other feral creatures
Curled like starfish slumbering in the loamy ground

I have sent it someplace black,
where no stars splash across the horizon

Where everything is secret and has a story
Where only roots and the quiet

tracks of deer can be heard
I have sent all that aching to a place of trees

marked by seeds and slow-moving worms—
I have hidden it well; you will never find it.

Reading Room

As you sleep, lenticular clouds cross overhead.
They lie on their backs blocking the Sangre de Cristo mountains.

Your face contains a hundred different kinds
Of clouds—soaring cumulus, sun-silvered mackerel,

a smear of slow-moving cirrus, nimbostratus swollen with rain.
Your palette's filled with blues:

robin's egg, flax, blue bonnet, violent thunderhead,
A barn owl dive-bombing its prey.

You breathe in indigo; you breathe out violet-blue
air stinging with the scent of lilacs in summer.

You dream of hawks. A bonded pair stretches and floats
On a small river of wind, bee pollen dusting their wings.

Clouds speckle your face as I watch you.
Each cloud a syllable, a line, a story, a word.

I long to read the cloudy tea leaves trailing after
You as you emerge from sleep, groggy, hair a mess.

I long to read the Braille of your skin and know you.

Bucket List

If you want to see the love of your life, look in the mirror.

You want to wear a falconer's glove and stare into the fierce eyes of a sparrowhawk perched on your wrist. You want to feel that strange wild beauty well up inside you. You want to make risotto and watch the onions soften in the pan, adding broth and silken pebbles of rice slowly, so the house fills with its fragrance as the mixture simmers. You want to kiss a lover's mouth until the blood rushes to your face. You want to learn to play the ukulele and draw human faces in charcoal and pencil. You want to trace your tenderness back to its roots. You want to watch the blue rivers of time pooling in your tired eyes. You want to walk the El Camino de Santiago and feel those pilgrim stones pass under your feet, feel the souls of everyone who's ever crossed over them. You want to watch a raven rest on a fence post outside the kitchen. You want to lie on your back and ponder the rose of Venus blinking in the distance. You want to walk the labyrinths of Machu Picchu, ghosts hovering in the mist, miles above sea level, while you untangle your history. You want to burrow into your bed in winter and warm your feet.

There is no other place other than where you are.

If you want to find the life of your life, dig here.

Open the inner door in the center of your chest and step inside.

There you'll find everything you need.

Mother

A pearlescent moon rises, like a white kite at dawn

Her crown a tangle of sheets knotted high,

She's an empress, a Contessa, a card sharp,

A map of a strange unknown land

Demeter

After her daughter's abduction,
Field upon field of grain rotted
Apples fell from trees &
Turned to sweet, vinegary mush

Fires swept through boreal forests
And the oceans howled in agony
Mother Earth cracked into
spidery fissures & cow's milk ran dry

All greenness soured
All crops died on the farm &
Fish forgot how to swim
Home to spawn

All that is lush
Turned to mulch
Turned to rot
Turned to bile

Nothing grew anywhere
While the black moon
Furiously chanted
Persephone's name

Aidan

For Elissa

On shore, an egret stands on one leg,
Awaiting her next meal

Ponderosas check the morning air
As you slip, head-first into life

Your mother's heart sits beside her as
Currents of silt, mud, twigs

Show her the way back into her body; you cry
Then quiet to the sound of her voice

A boy with indigo hair, an open
Face and suede blue feet, your

Torso marked with salt lines
From the Strait of Juan de Fuca

Your mother loses herself in the blur of the moment
Your eyes riddled with lenticular clouds, blink & drizzle

A seal pup to nip her hand
As blood smears the salty water

Lilith

A night-bird,
Banished

A witch-demon
Singing

An ex-wife
Fleeing—

A snake charmer
A screech owl

A truth-teller
A strawberry moon child

A woman on the verge
Of immolating

At the stake
For simply

Telling the truth
Lilith

Death & rebirth
The scraping of the womb

The cauterized,
often dead wound

The howling
She-wolf

Uvalde, Texas

Imagine
a small dark-eyed girl
A red petunia, a meadowlark

Dialing 911: *Send help. Please.*
We need help.
He. Has. A. Big. Gun.

In the hallway
Outside the classroom-
Turned slaughterhouse

The police fumble
With their phones
And call for more vests

More rifles & bullets
More backup
More armor

They wait & wait
As other children
Shout out

We're here! We're—
And gunfire erupts again—
And silence follows

While hundreds of officers
wait some more
One teacher dies

On the phone with her husband:
I love you—I love you—I—
Children scattered around her

Smeared with blood
& brain matter
and

a good guy with a gun

Never comes

Elegy for a Finch

She asks me why the tiny finch died
Why she found it, small feet curled over
Lying on its back in the dirt

She wonders if it ate too much seed
Or died of thirst
Or scalded its throat

On wildfire smoke
thirty miles away
Clearly visible from here

Did this finch fall from the sky?
Or did its bird-let heart
Choke and simply stop?

She buries it the next morning
Digs a body-sized hole
In the soft soil between some iris bulbs

I hear her mournful prayer
For its small life
As she covers its feathers

Its gray beak
The unruly tuft on its head
And pats its grave with her open palm

Jellyfish

The night washes silver
Water through an open door

Her shoulders
Sprout magpie's wings

She keeps a jar of starfish and sea glass
On her windowsill

Her hair twisted with ribbons, twigs,
And tiny, jeweled threads

Her body, a withered peach,
Naked breasts like pale moons

Grackles circle in
Cascading rivers of night

Her ovum, luminescent jellyfish
Nap quietly above her fallopian tubes

Dreaming in Karbala

In the Black Hawk
on the way back to the base
Medics worked on what was left of me.
Floating in a river of morphine,
I stood beside my body and observed the space
Where my right hand used to be.
I felt the wind whip through the chopper
As it flew low, rotors grinding and spinning
I smelled the burnt smear,
My face had become.

I trust ER docs will cut and paste me back together.
A paper, wax, and glue soldier:
No right clavicle, no interior vein
No index finger, no thumb.
They'll wrap my arm in bandages
After they cauterize the improvised,
explosive, aftermath…

The whole while I will dream of my wife
Her back tight against me
The baby still nursing at her breast
Smelling of powder and milk
Eyes fluttering as sleep takes her.
My hand will rest on her white thigh
as I draw phantom flowers on her bare skin.

I will pray she never stirs, never sees,
never wakes to see how things have changed.

The Widowed Bride

You came home—but
You didn't

Your body arrived
On an overnight transport—not dead

But not alive, either.
Floating between this world

And the next one,
In a ghost world only you

can find. You're buried
In this dead flesh

My body's become.
You're furrowing deep,

Your beak into my breastbone
& these pendulous breasts

Only your baby daughter
Still touches.

I've absorbed you into the womb
You recall loving, once.

You are a father in name only.
You are not here, and

not there, either.
I look for you

But I don't know
how to find you.

You never left *there*: the burn pits
The stench of constant death

The unspoken words
Stuck, as though

an arrow pierced
Straight through your throat.

I remember asking my father
about WWII once.

About his experience
In the South Pacific

During the days and weeks
Before Hiroshima & Nagasaki

Rained indiscriminate hell
on women, children, bees,

butterflies, buildings
factories & grandfather trees.

He was slow to reply,
Cigarette smoke engulfed his face.

"I did a lot of things I'm not proud of.
Let's leave it at that."

He's been dead
Nearly twenty years now.

Those decades open like fissures
After an earthquake.

Two blurred decades
Since I became an orphan.

And now,
Empty time stretches out

As far as this widowed bride
Can see.

The Patron Saint of Lost Things

For Julianne – November 28, 1956 – September 20, 2022

On the last night of summer,
In the azure twilight before the Equinox moon

As light and darkness balanced on the lip of the horizon
The world released you from its arms

And your heart slowed and stopped, hushing you—
Shushing its rush of blood

And as it did, you remembered what
it felt like to be weightless—

To no longer ache in your joints and fingers
And you dropped your fleshy roundness

Like a cerulean dress made of gauze
And stepped into the deepest windows of sky

All your life
You collected lost things:

Cats of all stripes and colors,
forlorn men, lost girls, hungry children

All of them burrowed into your open arms
And found a home there, never wanting to leave

You collected exotic flavors, philosophies,
Snippets of hymns, Yeats poems

You longed to save wanderers, freaks,
homeless girls, & litter upon litter of kittens

But never yourself,
never yourself—like

Your favorite saint, Gertrude
You surrounded yourself as she did,

With dozens of cats,
your door always open,

House, an abandoned shoe
Filled to overflowing

You cut yourself into bite-sized
Pieces to feed others

As alms, as offerings, as penance
As prayers for the world's redemption

You gave yourself away, every cell,
Every fiber, every bit of bone

You gave it all away—
And when you finished

You ate your last meal,
Down to that last crumb and

You settled on the sofa,
Arms slack, TV on,

The sound turned down,
As you quietly went to sleep

Skin stiffening, blood pooling
Mouth turning blue

As your face folded in
like a bluebird's wing

And you took

     your
            leave

Dangerous Things

You keep a suitcase
Full of monstrous words
And poisonous, slithering
verbs under your bed

You slide in fresh dictionary entries
Snapping the lid shut
As it shimmers and shakes
& Gnashes its teeth, mouth filled with

Glistening scarabs and salty
Fibonacci seashells,
Dried roses & rusty keys
To unknown doors

Poems are dangerous things
They reveal your scars, your raw
Wounds, the gaping bullet holes
Blown through the back of your head

Poems are damning creatures—
Creatures who stalk your sleep
And slash your face, pull your hair
With their sharp hook-like hands

You keep these creatures
Hidden: out of sight,
out of mind,
Out of line, out of time

Pebbles & feathers & entrails
Your tender liver & aching spleen
You take these in your hands
Whenever you write

A single line

Our Lady of Being Done with the Back of the Bus

In memory of the indomitable Rosa Parks

No is a
complete sentence.

I've arrived at
No.

See,
Like you, I am *tired.*

No, I will not
give up my seat.

Instead,
I will endure

days and weeks
and months

Of long walks
Home.

Of bone weary
but resolute, *No.*

I will endure
Blistered, aching feet

& the vitriol
Of raging voices

& vicious dogs,
Yellow spit and fire hoses

Stomping &
Screaming: N—

I will survive all this
Before I ever

Stop saying

No.

Day of the Dead/Día de los Muertos

For Momma

Without warning without desire without owning that each life draws not just a first breath (filling up, up) but a last one, too. without soaking in rain without drinking to hide without thirst for stars without thimbles and thread without solid flesh reminding me without tea and milk without silken hair pinned up in a French knot without fierce gazes without rooms full of geriatric cats and drooping houseplants without mist rising off a waterfall, what is this life? Without raw hands and tiny stitches without crazy quilts made of fancies from the button box without embroidery and newspaper clippings without *"the devil's in the details"* without *"Día de los Muertos"* skeletons without ginger cake molasses and curling ribbon without African masks without Buddha's compassion without Black Madonna hidden in a painted cave without Frida and Diego's fighting without tapas and raspberry beer without Nana's Christmas cactus blooming in the window in Winslow, Arizona without freight trains and Slim Jims without the silver glint of teeth without terminal breast cancer without the angel of death hovering without numinous darkness shifting behind an aspen grove without sour cherry pie without swirling prayers without Zuni bracelets and pointed birthday hats without lemons eaten with salt without respite without wanting without books spilling words, letters drifting and dancing without ashes falling into Puget Sound without salmon returning to spawn without saguaros hosting lizards and ravens without the clattering of dishes breaking and the slicing of fingers without the rush of Hannah Creek without my childhood bed without peals of laughter without telephone lines buzzing under our braided voices without collage and Baba Yaga's house without white candles dripping without mystery without Jung and dreaming mandalas without twisting labyrinths without God without lush brush strokes without steady breath rising and falling without a ticking heart without your voice calling me to dinner without death's long jagged shadow—

no life

Meditation on Returning to Your Wildness

rose petals underfoot,

their scent stuck

to her feet,

her hands—she

moves through the forest

lightning fast

an unknown, starving

feral creature

Colorado City

She dreams of the slots in Water Canyon
Fills her pockets with striated stones
Empties her chest cavity
Searching for lost seed beads—

She sees herself in murky water
a blank tree, budding branches cup the sky
She wades in, turning slowly,
soaks her lungs, fills her raw throat—

She floats on her back a while
Skirts shadowing stones slick with moss,
an avalanche of leaves and light
spatter and flag her ankles and arms

No option other than motherhood
baby at her breast every eighteen months
until her womb
      —that unruly copperhead—

slips out on the birthing table
Leaving her hemorrhaging,
A perforated placenta staining her narrow white bed
The color of ripe pomegranates

June Cleaver: Sit Down and Shut Up

She handled me in the same way she was *handled*,
With the brusque fingers of hard work,
With callused palms & critical eyes watching,
waxing, ironing, primping & frosting each exacting meringue.
She learned to mix and pour a perfect vodka gimlet,
Batter a mouth-watering Southern fried chicken,
And bake sweet cherries jubilee by the age of twelve.

There are things you must know, she tells me,
the world expects more of a girl. You must
Learn to cut lemons, julienne carrots
& Sautee onions until they're golden brown.
You must relentlessly train yourself to
flatten your affect & break your own branches
so your husband can see the sky.

You need to measure salt
& baking soda in the palm of your hand.
You must militantly fold sheets
to create crisp hospital corners.
As the daughter of a daughter
You must know these things.
I would be remiss in not preparing you.
A girl needs all this

                    to

                              survive.

Sylvia's Lost Note

Drop a coin in the slot
And light a candle for me

After you find me fallen, a white birch,
A snow-covered corpse outside the ovens at Dachau

After you listen to our babies
Wailing in the starless, winter air

Our flat's windows open deep into the night
While you were out fucking some whore

These years of our marriage
Me cow heavy with children

Umbilicus anchored in my solar plexus
Weight pinning me to the earth

Words for babies line up in a tidy row:
They'll be better off without me

A mother—screams barely muffled—
By the pillow she holds over her own face

No one sees the green-stick fractures
The way you clip my branches, one by one

Explain it to them, will you—
I want to stop breathing—in, out

Stop scratching, eking out a life, slow
Bones bristling, body aching—so

I drop this broken wren inside a bell jar,
My spirit a stillborn baby wrapped up tight

Marking this day, this gift
As your last

Letter from Gaia

I

To make just one bowl of shark fin soup
Half a dozen sharks off the coast of South Africa
Are pulled from freezing water
To the deck of a trawler

Once there, their fins are
Sliced off with a knife
And their bodies thrown overboard
Where they sink like paperweights,
No longer able to swim
Birth waters folding in around them—

II

The honor guards
Fold the red, white, and blue
Into a perfect triangle
And place it on the dark folds
Of her lap: it sits
Silently in the space
Where a grandchild should be—

III

On a factory farm in North Carolina
A sow nurses a dozen muddy piglets
Outside a million gallons of pig slough
Smells of ammonia and shit
As it poisons the groundwater.

Advertisers beg us to
Try the other white meat
Their teeth sharpened and white
On the flickering television screen.

IV

A witch doctor outside Pretoria tells his client
That sex with an infant two months or younger
Will clear up his bad blood.

V

Buddhist monks in red and gold robes
Draped in garlands of orange marigolds
Walk the streets of Myanmar
Holding incense sticks
While they chant—
Broken syllables cool in their mouths
As gunfire erupts.

VI

Alongside San Francisco Bay
Tides murmur as they lick the shore.
Dead herons wash ashore,
Their oil-soaked necks
Curved into a lamentation
Of loss.

Tributaries

For My Mother

1.
Chipped periwinkle
      Lady Slipper—
Bone teacup

Tarnished sugar tongs
      One cube please

Fingerprint smeared photo
Nana's handwritten note:
      Sailing for Savannah, 1928

2.
We stand on the moist dirt
Above her headstone
Lichen and moss scaling
The grooves of an inscription

I run my squat fingers over
A Braille remnant of a life:

Leo Trella Moon
November 15, 1878 – November 13, 1902
Beloved Daughter
Wife and Mother
Taken too soon

3.

From my grandmother's notebooks:

"…Hitch dat mule up to de cart
Drive him round some sinner's heart
Pharaoh's army all got drowned
Mary, don't you weep

Mary don't you weep, don't you moan
Mary don't you weep, don't you moan
Cause Pharaoh's army all got drowned
No, Mary don't you weep

4.

Ceanothus in bloom, deer
Munching on its buds

5.

Sarah lay in her crib
Watching the wall
Darkening, shifting—
Outside oaks dropped their leaves
Like Chinese fans littering
The streets of Montgomery

6.

Starlings gather
Each spring in Glastonbury
Fill the trees with 100,000 wings
Swaying,
Whipping,
Diving,
A disembodied velvet cape
That will soon cover
The world

7.

Nana kept Little Mother's braid
Wrapped in light tissue paper
In the bottom of her hope chest.

That brown-blonde braid
Passed to my mother when Nana
Died of breast cancer—

A stillborn strand of DNA
It lay in my mother's bedroom
For another fifty years

Until she finally donated it
To a cancer charity

8.

I never grew tired
Of seeing the giraffe,
Monkey, elephant
Trapped on the bottom of
My favorite cereal bowl

9.

Momma often lost herself
Listening to the soft
Cadence of her mother's voice

Nana's cigarette glowing,
Lips the color of American beauties
Her hands fluid, white birds

Shifting, dancing
As she smoked, drank
Rivers of thick, dark coffee

Spilled words into that
Container of warm air, you
Could almost hear an old Smith-Corona

Under her fingertips—
A bell ringing each time
She finished a line

10.

A plastic Easter egg full of jellybeans
                  My name painted
                                 Like a ribbon across the top

11.

Santana sings
Of his father's death,
Of the way love continues
Moves

Mother and daughter
rock and sway
In the thick air

Our feet lift off the dusty floor
As we dance

12.

On her 73rd birthday
She visited Del Ridge Way in Burien
Retracing the route
She walked to grade school in 1945

As snow fell in flakes, she stood
At what had been a tangle of woods—
She wept, looking at the creek bed
A smattering of trees bearing witness

She told me that weekend,
Coffee in our cups growing cold
The buzz of the telephone line between us:

I was overwhelmed by a longing for my mother—

13.

        Horsehair brush
    Demitasse cup shaped like a strawberry
        Pale colored wine glasses with twisted stems

14.

According to anthropologists
Elders greeted each new child
Face still slick
With after birth
Saying:
We love you and support you
On your journey

When death came
Tribal members—their faces covered
With hundreds of tributaries
Knelt and whispered as breath stilled:
We love you and support you
On your journey

15.

Canyon de Chelly—sand, rock
Curving thigh

Dry grass biting her leg
As her feet trace

The trail, loose gravel
Open fist

Under this sky
She is three years old again

Under this sky
She is smart, invisible

Under this sky
No split lip, spilt milk

This smoldering place
Cannot be erased

Still resting tick-tight
In her marrow

16.
"Our pets greet us
When we cross to the other side,"
I say, knowing this will comfort my mother

Her animal companions
Her constant familiars
Light her days

I imagine a room of soft light
And the sound of a small stampede
As dozens of cats cross to meet her

Tails up, faces expectant—Calico, Manx,
Tabby, tuxedo, marmalade

They rub their faces against her warm legs
As though they never left her

17.
The sound of a faucet dripping

Nana sent my mother
      To the kitchen for a glass of water

I stood in the doorway only weeks
Past my fourth birthday, watching

      As she rose off the bed

      Spirit light as gauze

18.

I call my mother
To tell her
My longtime boyfriend
Fucked my best friend

    Sharp intake of breath

God, I hoped it would be different for you.

19.

A flaw is purposely
Woven into every Navajo rug
        To let the spirit out

20.

I wrap my arms around
Her weathered body,

    Kiss her forehead

    I think about a bolt of fabric
        Tomato red, gold, cobalt
Strands of thread taut between us

There is no knife

    Sharp enough

      To sever them

Tsunami

For J

Your face turned bluish gray &
You died right in front of me
A dinner of roast beef and potatoes,
peas spilling from your fork
as it dropped from your hand

Your fingers claw-like,
mottled with age
as your blood
Stopped—abruptly & congealed
in the pools of your lungs

You stopped breathing
And a tsunami hit the
Glass of this high rise
Shattering it and giving way
as I drowned beside you

As I watched my life drain
Through the cracks in the floor
You slack in your chair
Water—everywhere I looked
So much filthy water

How can all these moments
Between us—years and
years and years—
a child, a long marriage,
our careers writ large,

The books
The articles,
shared cigarettes,
the sacred space
In our familial bed

How can it suddenly

Flatten into this?

Animal Dreams

Red rocks thrum and shake
Remind of that day in Oak Creek
Watching sparrows weave her a sweater

She undoes the ribbon to open her gift:
A cricket, a coin, a jumping bean
When she opens her mouth, tiny turtles slip out

His head elongates in the birth canal
Gravel in her throat tasting of gasoline
Her father's military photo watches from the mantle

As she curls into this animal softness
Pliable as a hide beaten soft with sticks
Her baby's head crowns

And she pushes him into his life

Blue Angel Writes to Tell Me

Last night in the shockwaves of a dream
That blue ghost I knew in London
Came to visit.
I am the pulse of your blood racing,
She laughed, dropped blueprints of my past
On the floor around my bed.

Starlings fluttered on telephone wires,
I remembered the crunch of April snow,
That morning snow, that turns to rain by noon.
The tea kettle whistled,
Put steam on the windows that ran in rivulets,
Sang: Are you coming home?

Green kernels of Spring
Unfolded like poppies
With no boundaries or words to confine them.
I felt as infinite as the sky.
Blue Angel shook me awake,
Tuned my ears to the hush of the pines

And wind blowing rough against the house.
I smelled rain and petrol.
A black cab waited outside,
Backseat full of roses red as Ida's lips and nails.
The stars came in an open window,
Sniggered: Will you be coming home?

I wandered out in my nightgown,
Walked over to the Serpentine,
Went wading.
Toward morning I found a bag of coins,

Threw them into the water
Wishing until they sunk into the slime.

This morning when I awoke,
I felt my thoughts migrating north
Over the pole toward some greener, sweeter bed.
My eyes sketched a map on the wall,
Felt a mother's kiss saying:
Come home, come home.

Crone

Strings of paper cranes dance in the courtyard
As a cat traces a figure-eight on her cheek

Minutes cascade into willows, & her
        Hands fill with lockets of ripening grain

Self Portrait

A woman with the head of a barn owl
Watches as this place trails smoke, & wildfires burn

She practices divination with a twig,
A finger bone, a blue lace agate

She paints the sky below, the ground above
Gizzards, bits, and bones dance on her dirty plate

She poses for an imaginary portrait—just then, just how—
Catches her animal softness, her sleek gleam, her sharp beak

As aspens open like umbrellas, leaves the color of saffron
She fills with wildness and wonder and what ifs

Because

Because you cannot remember what you just said.
Because letters, vowels, consonants leave you as soon as you speak.

Because when I look at your face,
I see the hard luck, hard life, hard start that stained you

Because you kept granddaddy in your life, for us,
even as he broke the yolk of all tenderness in you

Because you tell me, even now, you long to see your mother,
To hear her call you in, out of the woods in Burien, for supper.

Because she left you, ravaged by metastasized breast cancer
When I was only four & you were 29.

Because both your sisters and your younger brother
Have all taken their boats & crossed the river of death.

Because there's only you now, plaintive & bitter
Living in the frosting sting of late life.

Because I wanted something more than what you had
So, you label me as 'what, for you, might have been.'

Because I cannot find a way to help you see yourself as I see you:
Lush & wise, as all things are

When the last glow of life
Shimmers under the skin of everything

Because I want you to know
the sweetness hidden in our suitcase of sorrow

Because I want you to find the purpose
In the days you have left.

Because there's still time to love the world
To love the mackerel skies & the soil damp with rain

Because I came through you & you shaped me &

You did something good.

Witch Wife

Drop seeds that will sprout
Cultivate lavender & garlic

Sage & scotch broom
Fuji apples & Braeburns

Heirloom tomatoes &
Basil, oregano, thyme

Cast spells
That gather bees whose feet

Are heavy with pollen
And the marrow of the sunflowers

Outside the kitchen
Watch a hummingbird float

In the still air
The sun on her iridescent feathered throat

Talk to the cottonwoods, the scratch oaks
The pines and the mesquite

Give them your regards &
Profound thanks

For watching over this place
For giving us clear air to breathe

For cooling us
As we sit in the balm of their shade

Greet all living beings
Bow to their graceful tender rootedness

Realize they are
Your kindreds

Invocation

I call on you
when I need a stiffer spine
A boiling rage

To cauterize
A wound
A lashing

A hanging
A terrifying
wrong

I call on your vivid blue light
In the still spinning darkness
Of my own death & rebirth

I call your name
When I feel most alone
Most forsaken

Most gutted
By the world
In which women

Are ghosts
And livestock
Awaiting slaughter

I call on your tender
Fierce remembrance
Of what I am—

You come
Wearing bracelets of neck bones
And skirts of jangling skulls

You come, tiny conch shells
decorating your ankles
A severed man's head in one hand,

A bloodied knife in the other
You remind me, this subjugation
of the feminine, the life of this life

Will not stand

Skeleton Woman

As ravens circle above a dry field,
The horse smiles after she braids its tail
The woman sees her father's reflection
Whenever she studies the rains

Blue rivers spill out of her mouth
as she sits still on the bed
Residual traces of her past
washing her in remembrance: a fleck of dead skin,

a cigarette butt, a well-worn rock n' roll t-shirt.
Palo Verdes sweep the horizon underground while
Her dog dreams of open onion fields, just turned &
The cat curls, chestnut small, in the flesh of her lap

A man sleeps hard next to her,
Her chiseled bones the cage that traps him
He thought he did the catching, the finding
The rescuing…

But she fished for him
She scouted the deep hunger in his eyes
And now, on dry land
he'll drown in his own bed

What if

My body was
A sacred wonderland
And I let myself deeply love
All my flaws, all my terrible
Mistakes & amputations?
What if I believed
In my own divinity
And stopped my doubts
In their tracks?

What I See

I see a weathered crow, folded wings
Her children, once shimmering ovum—
Dried chickpeas—strung into a garrote
Palo Verde longing for its phantom limbs

I see breasts, pale areolas slowly blinking skyward
Peripheral edema, a turtle's neck
Double chin riding her pubis,
Scar slashed above the tree line

I see residual cuts, tubes, probes
Lost surgical instruments stitched up
With men who left her
Meticulously mapped skin, tongue in her marrow

I see a gazelle's shoulders,
A mouth smeared with blood
Traces of a woman falling inside out
Tributaries, charcoal lines, a pencil sketch of her shattered limbs

I see everything lush, fragrant
Everything fractured
Everything polished, smoothed

I see a skin horse,

A thrumming hive,

A frayed overcoat beaten soft

Triage

Electrical wires lace the night.
She forgets her ticket, her passport, her suitcase of rags.

Her head's a bird house spilling suet and seed.
She wears red cowboy boots and a two-step skirt

A river pools under her dancing feet.
She can morph into a sleek green lizard or

an elephant holding her own tail.
Shakti. Lilith. Eve. Persephone.

Shekinah holding a bag containing
Medusa's head of writhing snakes.

Her blood, the rusty tang
Of her whole being

Lives inside each broken, yoked woman
As an inheritance & sacred bond.

Rosary

Face/Beloved

Cannot/She finds
She cannot

Recall the glimmering—
Silver braid

She lost to kitchen shears
After a round of chemo

Riverbed/corn silk/husk
Pollen cannot find its source

Trace its lines/breaks
Back to/flesh/flange

Count amber
Rosary beads

One for each moment
Dissolving in her charred throat

Count/One *Our Father*/Count
One Hail Mary, full of grace—

Hold each bead between
Her thumb and index finger

As though it contains
Her life itself

Bones

I am standing on bones:
The bones of a cancer-riddled uncle
A cousin's leukemia
An aunt's rotting cranium
My father's cracked rib cage.

I am standing on bones:
The bones of my son-of-a-bitch granddad
His swindles & gambles & tall tales
The slender bones of soup kitchen Nana
& her chain smoking daughter

I am standing on bones:
My slave-owning great, great, granddaddy
His prisoner-of-war brothers locked up at Gettysburg
Moon bones & Viking bones
& the bones of a confederate spy

I am standing on the bones
of John Adams in the 'new world'
& John Donne in the old; bones
Sheltered in cathedral vaults
With muted stained-glass windows

I am standing on the bones
Of witches & fools & whores
Tricksters, troublemakers & spinners of stories
Their delicate chalky bones scorched black
Lying wherever they fell.

Their broken skeletons long asleep in the wormy loam
Skeleton orchards, seeding & growing &
trickling up through time
Deliberately & resolutely marching in formation:
Until they find their way to me.

Burial

Boxes of primroses, remnants of salty ribbon
Earthworms catch in his teeth
                         bits of hair, dried saliva
Trampled in an earthy box

Potato bugs crawl out of his eye sockets
                 & the soft flesh of his mouth

Glisten like swallows' wings, like Hawkmoths, like sooty oil lanterns

Light flecks catch on the wind
                         beckon and un-spool stars

Dead at 40, his words still fist-tight in his chest

A rider-less horse, a Negro spiritual
         A dusty Old Testament, open to the 23rd Psalm

Mossy air thick
         With questions

                 & stomping

                 & shouting tears

Unraveling Baba Yaga

I

The crow medicine man raised one blue-black wing over the bird's small frame as she cowered on the floor. His voice erupted from his beak, its pebbly sound showering around her.

You have betrayed the order of the shapeshifters by revealing our powers to a human boy. You are therefore exiled to the birch wood of the far north, with only animal guides as companions.

The fire hissed as the medicine man spit his spell into the rising flames. One by one, moving around the circle in which she sat, tribal witnesses turned their backs on her. Shunned, she was now dead to every breed of bird. She would spend her life in human form, never again able to shape-shift and take to the sky.

In your new life, unruly, rotten, and lost human children will find their way to you. They will puzzle you with riddles you have no choice but to answer.

II

The human girl noticed her bruised arms and bare feet. A stranger here, she didn't recognize this, or any other, grove of trees. She awoke next to a rat terrier and a Manx. They sat a few feet away, regarding her with suspicion.

In the distance, a log cabin stood—its tin roof reflecting the moon.

She rose. Cat and dog followed suit. As she moved toward the cabin, it suddenly ducked into the trees and hid. Barking, Dog made chase. House ran deeper and deeper into the woods as the girl gave chase, too. Cat followed for a while, then slowed, then stopped. She washed her paws, sitting back, waiting patiently for an outcome.

House stood twenty yards or so away on two large chicken legs. It occasionally scratched at the dirt and circled as though settling itself into a nest. Desperate for a place to call home, the girl spoke the first words that came to her. In a soothing voice, she called *Turn your back to the forest, your front to me.*

The small house shifted to the north and nestled itself on the ground. A red door materialized, keyhole a mouth with sharp teeth. Without hesitation, the girl crossed the threshold. Once inside, she felt right at home.

III

A magic gate needs a password. What was hers?

The medicine man—yes, she remembered him now—had been right. Snot-nosed brats, runaways, ruffians, and ragamuffins found their way to her door. Their voices singed her ears with questions, riddles, and more questions. They sucked the marrow from her bones—

Early on she realized, for every kindness, every answer she gave, she aged a whole year.

Now, no longer a girl, or even a maiden, her face showed every tributary of middle age. Her hair hung in shanks around her face, peppered with gray.

These brats stole my life. They yanked my spirit loose of its tether, left me nothing but a shell.

She was especially rough on boys; boys who thought they could outwit her, or worse, make her love them. Poor fools. Tibia, fibula, femur, and patella formed pickets for her lovely white fence. Vacant skulls lined its edge, wind combing their sockets.

IV.

Face scuffed up as a dried apple,
> she drinks tea made of blue roses
>> and for an hour—maybe two—she's young again.

V.

Barely breathing, this last dreadful child's question upon her:

How can I find my way home?

Her throat, raw with phlegm, percolates an answer:

Die—

VI.

Cat and dog wrap her in a shroud, dragging her corpse outside to a hastily arranged funeral pyre.

House dances a jig beside a weathered birch whose roots feather deep into the forest.

Cat lights kindling, bits of string and fluff, leftover candle nubs, and oil from the bedside lamp. The fire leaps to life. As the crone's body sputters and starts to flame, an indigo bird emerges, eyes the color of polished rubies.

She whispers over a clamor of hissing and barking and flying fur:

In exile no more.

As Above, So Below

She often wonders why everyone can't see
The invisible world she harbors
Field upon field of altocumulus clouds
As far as her eye can see
The smell of dirt stuck to her fingers
After slipping as she walked
the muddy gully behind the house
Sky blue and black, black and blue
Branches silver with morning rain
She wonders if the sparrow-hawk wonders
Or if it simply acts from instinct
She wonders if what's she's planted even matters
Or if all her fierce, hard work
                              simply passed the time

The High Priestess

You often visit me
as I drift and dream, eyes flickering

as I watch bruised willows bend over
the water of the Rio Grande—there

I struggle to listen,
to hear the rainfall of

Your secret spiral,
& the singing bells you wear

At your throat
From which all language rises

I watch you, like a cat
Tail twitching, pupils enlarged

Your voice's rasp
bubbling up

To sever my delusion
And the idea that there is ever

Any distance between us
You walk beside me

Shaking and shimmering
Your rattle and stinger

Poised to bite,
teeth dripping potions

To jar me awake,
to make me conscious

Of life's mysteries
& this intuitive soul

That sometimes
slumbers through life

To show me
there's so much more—than

This

Clouds

As white carnations and freesia
Float on southbound currents
I count the days I may have left
with my mother, now confused by keys,
locks, kettles, closets & the random
movement of Cassiopeia.

She ruminates over photos,
papers her journals with images
to help stop her forgetting
everything and everyone.
When she opens her mouth,
she releases an unruly hive of cactus wrens
Her irises pool & swirl,
hazel centipedes filled with clouds

I often cannot find her—she's

                                    gone.

The River of Death

A desiccated dead cat sleeps near a barrel cactus
Bleached bones breaking through its skin

As she happens upon it,
Willows hold her in their arms, whisper: gentle, gentle

She traces the body with an imaginary marking pen
Makes a puppet with the paper

That night her dog rests in the small of her back
As she savors the sleek coffee of his coat with her free hand

Under her breath, she prays for all those crossing the Ganges,
their open funeral pyres flaming

She sends them a fellow night traveler:
a tabby hit by a fast gray car & a slow, blinking smear of taillights

Meditation on Letting Go

Moths dust their feet
On uncovered garlic bulbs

Chalk the porch with
pollen stuck on their wings

Moist, black earth
Sweetened by rain clouds

Leaves me swollen & bursting my banks
Let go, let it all go

Only what's yours will remain

This Way

Sunlight grazes frozen branches
Her jaw aches from swallowing words

In her dream, she travels
She can't recall where or why or what time

She pulls on a jangly skirt, dotted with sequins
As crickets catch in her throat

Ivy grows slowly up the ridge of her spine
Its green leaves flush with rain

She paints an arrow on her arm,
Following the line of her index finger

This way, this way

Descent into Madness

For Hart

I have to get through to God.
His number's right here. Can't you see it?
I keep dialing and dialing but there's no answer,
Just the sound of a thousand bees
Buzzing like jack saws in my elephant ear,
Then the slow hissing of a water snake
Instructing me from inside the cone of an ocean wave:
"Please hang up and try your call again."

To pass the time between conversations
I jot words upon words—
Floor-snot-cot-make-
door-root-roof-open-cave—
Pages and pages of knots and lines
heaped inside these ink-soaked notebooks.
I sit on the curb; talk myself out of the sky,
Talk myself down off a telephone wire
dancing with drunken ravens.

My brain is a luminous substation,
Full of intricate gridlines and magnetic ribbons,
blinking off and on, beneath the surface of this city.
As I pass a tree with five blazing eyes,
I scale the fence and grab hold
of 150,000 volts of pure blue-green transcendence.

God himself tells me:

You are the Christ.
You are the Resurrection.
You are the Holy Ghost.

Breadcrumbs

And your doubt can become
Your ally, your fierce reminder
Of every blackened backroad
Every barren stream and
Every long moment
you stumbled through life
in red shoes the size of thimbles
Shoes that cut the arches
Of your white feet and
Told you to
accept only breadcrumbs.
Never to gulp the hungry air
Or open the shutters in your chest
To reveal your lionheart
Your doubts used to be the tales
You spoke into dark stars under
The bright gaze of Venus
No more, dear heart.

No more.

Off with Her Head: The Dangerous, Divine Feminine Responds

"She is so bright and glorious that you cannot look at her face or her garments for the splendor with which she shines. For she is terrible with the terror of... avenging lightning, and gentle with the goodness of the... sun..."

— HILDEGARD VON BINGEN FROM *SCIVIAS*, III, 4.15, translated by Mother Columba Hart, O.S.B. and Jane Bishop

Vilified, gang-raped,
slaughtered, hung,
stripped, drowned, irradiated,
dismembered,
shot, acid-splashed
locked up, stoned,
beaten, strangled, infected,
impregnated, aborted,
abandoned, kicked,
run out of town,
molested, slashed,
marked, maimed, slammed,
terrorized, murdered, scarred,

     Left
          for
               dead
    A punchline
               Emphasis on 'punch'
                   Not line
    You've
                   chopped off her hands &
                   cut out her tongue to silence her

You've

                bound her feet
                until they became tiny white mice
                no good for running away

You've

                blackened her eyes,
                broken her bones,
                smacked her unconscious &
                smeared her body on the side of the road

Yet

Still

She rises

        like copper sap, like a sockeye salmon returning to spawn,
          like a field of sunflowers waving to passing cars

              She emerges
Queen bee-Kali,

all serve her & the delicate hive mind

        Soldiers march, feet sticky with her glow
           The green fuse of clover honey
                Born of each petal and tender leaf
Still

She gives birth

        She incubates, simmers, protects

            the iridescent seahorse tucked inside a mermaid's purse

Still

she dares,

she opens her mouth

      sings, whiskey-voiced, scented with rose water
          sings lost hymns & lullabies & childhood nursery rhymes

        She lights sandalwood, candles
        & remembers her dead
        marking her face with ashes

Witch, goddess, woman-child, crone
    warrior-woman, snitch, whore, scribe, maiden, artist, writer, mother—

She spins trickster tales, fool stories, & her own particular color of moonlight
  She brings on meteor showers & watches the sun slipping into sight again

Each day
    She flies—like a murmuration of starlings—
        Hair black, laced with silver
            Face indigo

She comes to me
    In the golden gray of a running dream

        shimmering and silent and full

Tell them, she says
Tell them I am in your bones,
your blood,
your soft tissue—
Tell them
      they cannot
kill me

Cygnus

"And I hunted only your larger selves that walk the sky."

—Kahlil Gibran

a ruby sea creature.
a sand dollar.
a bone orchard.
a carved music box.
a relay station.
a snow leopard.
a whiptail lizard.
an Apache plume.
A constellation:
Cygnus
The swan.
a patch of moonflower.
a white-tailed rabbit.
a greening patch of bear grass.
a holy fire.
a dying star.

Evanescent Creature

One day,
All this suffering
And wonder
And holiness
And strangeness

Will pass into *Ku*
A state of flux
Where energy
Still exists, but
Not here, not here

Where what made you, you
Will be erased
& will float like
a soft dandelion pappus
On a blustery Spring Day

Until you hear your mother's voice
Filling you with longing
Calling you back to the *Saha* world
To this realm of cause & effect & cause
Where you'll begin again.

Note: *Ku* is the Sanskrit word for sunya or sunyata. It roughly translates as the foundation of the universe, or the essence of each living thing. The Saha world is the 'mundane world' in which we live.

When the weariness of your day

feels like too much—
too much noise,
too much chatter,
too much, unsettled darkness.
Remember
Even oak trees rest, even the dry grasses
beneath your feet sleep
even the snow falling, feather-light,
each flake completely different from the last,
slows down, swirls in the clear air,
& Comes to rest on your eyelashes
If you need to breathe, breathe
If you need to sleep, sleep
If you need to pause, pause
Focus on the smallest sliver of time
Focus on the whorls
Stamped concentrically on your fingertips
Focus on that white scar on your left knee
The world will wait for you to catch up.

Acknowledgements

Both of my parents, who supported my creativity in their own ways.

Helen Simondet, who wrote me letters when I was a child and taught me to love words.

Ted Askew—who championed my creative work for 50+ years and has been the sounding board I've turned to since I was 17. Also, my first love, beta reader, & one of my oldest friends.

With fond memories of my time at the Centrum Poetry Foundation (1974–1976).

The long defunct, *Bellingham Bay Monthly*, which published my first poems in 1977 and paid me 50 bucks for the privilege.

And, finally, to my dear friend, Julianne White who died while I was compiling/writing this collection.

Also, the teachers who shaped me as a writer:

In memory of my high school English teacher, Helen Steele.

Robert Beath, who taught me to love learning.

Noel Riley Fitch, my master's thesis advisor.

Norman Dubie, who taught me to cut and prune ruthlessly.

Beckian Goldberg, who opened my eyes to new ways into the work.

Alberto Rios, who helped me see & explore magical realities.

Jeannine Savard, who arrived when I needed her.

Nelson Bentley, for encouragement and opening the door to poetry.

Robert Huff, for his gruff demeanor that toughened me up,

& Gladys Cardiff, who was the first published poet who saw something good in my work.

About the Author

SHAVAWN M. BERRY is a writer of poetry, prose, essays, & stories, an empath, an elephant lover, a dendrophile, and a stargazer. She considers herself a curator and creator of beauty. The core themes of her writing are human connection, empathy, and healing [spiritually and physically]. Her writing has appeared in Golden Dragonfly Press's, *Goddess; Sable Books' anthology, Red Sky—Poetry on the Global Epidemic of Violence Against Women; The Urban Howl; Trickster Literary Journal; The Huffington Post (HuffPo 50); elephant journal; The Good Men Project; Rebelle Society; Be You Media Group; Olentangy Review; Journey of Heart: Women's Spiritual Poetry; Black Fox Literary Magazine; The Cancer Poetry Project 2; Kinema Poetics; Kalliope; Poet Lore; California Quarterly; Westview—A Journal of Western Oklahoma; Meridian Anthology of Contemporary Poetry; North Atlantic Review; Concho River Review; Synapse; Living Buddhism; Blue Mountain Arts/SPS;* and *Poetry Seattle,* to name just a few. She's been writing about spirituality & healing & the divine feminine for more than forty years and has been a practicing Buddhist for the past 38 years. In 1998, she received her Master of Professional Writing (MPW) from the University of Southern California in Los Angeles where she specialized in Creative Nonfiction and Memoir. In addition to her work as a writer, she is an award-winning teacher, teaching writing courses full-time at a university in the desert Southwest. She lives in Albuquerque, NM with six cats and one lovely old dog as her constant companions.

Made in the USA
Coppell, TX
01 April 2023